Nature Walks in

DORSET

—— VOLUME II ——

NORTH & EAST

W0007549

Nature Walks in
DORSET
— VOLUME II —
NORTH & EAST

Tim Goodwin

DORSET BOOKS

First published in Great Britain in 1999

British Library Cataloguing-in-Publication Date
A CIP record for this title is available from the British Library

ISBN 1 871164 65 6

DORSET BOOKS
Official publisher to Dorset County Council
Halsgrove House
Lower Moor Way
Tiverton EX16 6SS
Tel: 01884243242
Fax: 01884 243325

Printed and bound in Great Britain by WBC Limited, Bridgend

CONTENTS

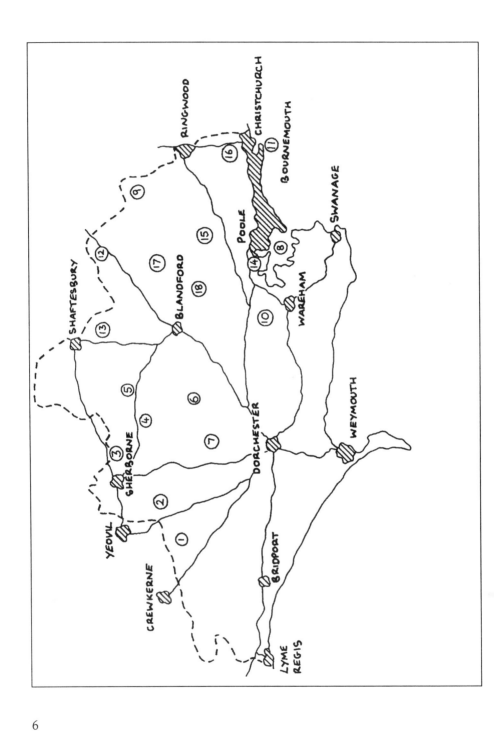

INTRODUCTION

This book is a companion volume to my *Nature Walks in Dorset, South and West* (also published by Dorset books). I have divided the county in two by using a rough line between Wareham and Crewkerne, and the walks in this book are all north and east of this line.

North and East Dorset offer a huge variety of natural habitats, from the great Dorset heaths, with their rare birds, plants and reptiles, to the chalk downs and their butterflies and herbs. River valleys offer a rich habitat for birds in the winter and summer alike: the Dorset woodlands provide easier sightings of three species of wild deer than almost any other in the country; while the superb estuarine environments of Poole and Christchurch Harbours pick up fascinating rarities every year.

Dorset has become famous in wildlife terms for the recent colonisation of the elegant and beautiful Little Egret. This exotic bird, which has never nested in Britain before, can be seen in many places in this book, and at almost any time of year. Places to search them out include Brownsea Island, Upton Country Park, Christchurch Harbour, and the water meadows around Shapwick. They can even be seen by major roads, for example the A31 south of Wimborne.

The walks in this book vary from 3 miles to around 9 miles, mostly in the middle of that range, and so provide roughly a half day's walking. They have been designed to be as varied, and evenly scattered over the region as possible, and all have been worked out with drivers in mind, so most are circular, though this has not always proved possible.

The descriptions are not, of course, anything more than pointers to the variety of natural history that can be seen, and you will undoubtedly see birds, plants, animals and insects that I have not mentioned – and miss one or two that I have. Clearly field guides helping to identify birds, butterflies and flowers would be useful. There are also notes about nearby pubs and places of refreshments, and in some cases other sights that can be seen on the walks

Sketch maps are provided on a scale of roughly 1:50,000, but walkers are strongly recommended to purchase relevant maps in the OS Explorer or Outdoor Leisure series for more detailed information.

1

HALSTOCK

HOW TO GET THERE

From the A356 by Wynyards Gap Inn, take the turning to Halstock. Follow the road, forking right, then left. Just past the turning to Higher Halstock Leigh is Winford Cottage on the left. On the right is a gate, with a nature reserve sign. Park there, and go through the gate. OS Explorer Map 117. Grid reference: ST514074.

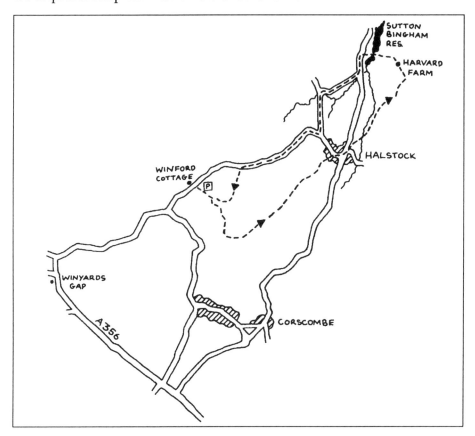

LENGTH
About 8 miles. Best in spring or summer.

THE WALK
Follow the track to Brackett's Coppice, a Dorset Wildlife Trust nature reserve, where the paths are often wet and muddy. Look out for Squirrels, Tits, Speckled Woods, Wood Anemone and the unusual Bird's Nest Orchid. Take the straight track, then curve sharp right down the hill. There is Bugle, Violet, Wild Strawberry, Wood Spurge, and fungi in autumn. Deer and Woodpeckers are frequent. After 200 yards swing left downhill, and cross the bridge. Check the stream for Kingfisher, Grey Wagtail and Dipper.

Over the stream, climb the hill and cross a stile, continuing straight with an open meadow on the right. Jays are frequent in the Oaks, and there are a variety of moths. Three different species of Fritillary butterflies can be seen. Cross another stile, and take the middle way. Willow and Garden Warblers, Blackcaps, and Chiffchaffs all visit, and Wood Warblers are possible. The path slants right, overhead Buzzards display, Sparrowhawks and Tawny Owls are fairly common. Honeysuckle can have White Admirals, and there are Dormice present. Continue straight, emerging from the reserve by another sign.

Turn right along the public footpath. In the hedges are Yellowhammers, Primroses, Bugle, and a few Spotted and Butterfly Orchids. The thickets can contain Lesser Whitethroat. Continue up the path, through a gate and turn left along Common Lane, a track. Cuckoos call throughout May. The hedges have Alder Buckthorn, Field Maple, Hawthorn, Hazel, Bryony, Vetch. Butterflies include Green-veined White, Orange Tip, Common Blue and Skippers. Where the track divides, turn left, down the hill, past spreads of Dog's Mercury. Bullfinches slip through the trees, and Holly Blues investigate Ivy.

Continue straight to the road, with the golf club on your left. Turn right into Halstock with many Swallows overhead, swing left in the centre of the village. Turn right – signposted Closworth – and immediately left along a dead end lane, with Ferns, Celandine and Finches. Cross a stream, with Pond Skaters on the pools, and turn left over a waymarked stile. The stream is on the left, with huge Mayfly hatches, dragonflies, including Golden-ringed, and both species of Demoiselle. Cross the meadow to the stile, then cut diagonally right over the next field, thick with Lady's Smock, to another stile. Cross a small trickle, and cut across another field to a waymarked stile in the far right corner. Cross it, turn right, then immediately left by another waymark. Go through the gate into another field, crossing it diagonally right to another gate, then turning left to follow the line of the hedge. There are many Buzzards overhead. Cross the stile at the end through a thin strip of woodland, then turn right and follow the waymarks to the bridleway.

Turn left on the bridleway and follow it to Harvard Farm. Turn left just before the farm, and go down the hill, following waymarks to the causeway over the southern tip of Sutton Bingham reservoir. Watch for Geese, Lapwing, Snipe, Duck, and Dabchick. In autumn there is a chance of Terns. Butterflies include Brimstone, Red Admiral. Cross the causeway, and continue straight to the road. Turn left. The roadside has Hedge Garlic, Ground Ivy. There are Whitethroats, Yellowhammers, and Linnets.

After a short distance turn right on a minor road. Peacock butterflies lay eggs on the Stinging Nettles. Follow it to Legg's bridge, turn left and follow the lane past the church. At the road junction turn right to Halstock Leigh. The hedgerow is thick with flowers – Stitchwort, Herb Robert, Red Campion, Honeysuckle, Speedwells, Dog Rose, a few patches of Wild Privet. Cuckoos call in late spring. Orange Tips and Green-veined Whites fly round Cow Parsley, which has bright orange Soldier beetles on it.

Follow the road about a mile, past Neville Farm, then just before Leigh Farm turn left by a waymarked stile. Continue straight, following the waymarks, with the hedge on your right. The fields have Hares and Foxes. Go through a gate into the edge of a wood, with a wire fence on your right. Look for Primrose, Celandine, Water Mint, and animal tracks in the soft earth. Turn right by the nature reserve sign, and continue straight. Nuthatches are frequent.

Turn right by a lone Ash tree with an obscured waymark about 100 yards before a shed. Continue straight up a ride, marked by yellow-painted posts, looking for Orchids, Twayblades, Deer, Scabious, Woodpeckers. In an opening by a single Silver Birch with a platform built on it, turn left and follow the path as it gradually curves to the right down the hill, entering a swathe of Ransoms. Cross the bridge, then continue straight up the hill and along the track, emerging by your car.

REFRESHMENT
Wynyards Gap Inn. The Post Office stores at Halstock.

2

YETMINSTER

HOW TO GET THERE
Park near the station.
OS Explorer Maps 129 & 117. Grid reference: ST598108.

LENGTH
6^1/$_2$ miles.

THE WALK
From Yetminster station, turn right up by the engineering firm, and follow the footpath sign to Beer Hackett up a muddy lane. The stream on the right has Chiffchaff in the trees, Garden Warbler in the thickets,

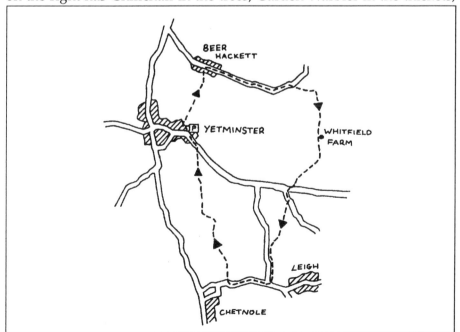

Iris, Demoiselle damselflies, and butterflies. Cross a stile and continue beside the stream until you come to a narrow footbridge on the right. Cross it, and then the railway track. There are Blackcaps in the trees. Cross the next field diagonally to the left, over another footbridge. The field has Snipe and a chance of Green Sandpiper in winter.

Swing left and follow the footpath straight towards Beer Hackett church, over more stiles. Cuckoos patrol the area in May and June. Finally pass through a kissing gate, with the church on your left. Turn right along the road. The village gardens attract Red Admiral, Peacock, Painted Lady and Comma butterflies. The ancient hedgerows of Blackthorn, May, Dog Rose, Maple, Hazel, Ash, and Alder Buckthorn are crawled over by Bryony, Ivy and Traveller's Joy. There are one or two patches of Meadow Cranesbill. The ditches have water plants. Watch for Yellowhammers, Whitethroats, Goldfinches, Spotted Flycatchers.

At Higher Knighton Farm, where the road swings left uphill, continue straight along a dead-end road, following it round to the right. Yellow Archangel grows in the hedge, there is a rookery in the wood, and Kestrels and Woodpeckers are frequent. Bittersweet and Water Forget-Me-Not grow in the wet ditch, with a variety of umbellifers, roamed by several species of beetle. Continue through Whitfield Farm yard, with many goats, then beside a wood. As the wood ends on your left, turn right by the yellow waymark and cross the field, with Pheasants. At the edge of the wood in front, the waymarked post has fallen, but the path through the wood is pretty clear.

Whitfield West Wood has a fine selection of the commoner flowers, including swatches of Bluebell, Violet, Primrose, and Wood Anemone, together with varied fungi. The old Oaks have Polpody ferns growing in them. There is a chance of Silver-Washed, Marsh and Small Pearl-Bordered Fritillaries, and several species of day-flying moths. At the end of the wood, cross the stile and straight over the next field to a way-marked stile, and then on to the road.

14

Turn right over the bridge, then left marked Leigh. About 100 yards on, turn right along a footpath. There is a part-flooded copse on the left, where ducks nest and there are many frogs in spring. Cross the way-marked stile at the end, then continue straight, with the hedge first on your left, then right. Roe Deer are frequent. Turn right at the end of the field, then rapidly left, crossing Church Lane by the waymarks. There is a small brook with Watercress, Large Red, Blue Tailed and Azure damselflies, Sedge Warblers, Wagtails. Continue over the next field, with the hedge on your left, cross the stile at the end, with the brook on your left. Turn right along the top of the next field, go through a way-marked gate, and then turn left on the by-road. The hedges are thick with Honeysuckle.

Turn right along the main road, with the usual hedgerow plants and birds, and Brimstone, Orange Tip and Green-Veined White butterflies. Fieldfare and Redwing comb the fields in winter. Just before Chetnole, turn right up Herbury Lane track with views and animal tracks in the mud. After a little over half a mile, where the farm track swings right into a field, cross the waymarked stile on the left, near a huge old Oak tree which sometimes has Purple Hairstreak butterflies. Follow the path straight across the middle of the field, then cross a waymarked stile on the far side, and cross a bridge, with dragonflies, including Golden-Ringed, Alderflies etc. The Wriggle River, like other streams in the area, provides a chance of seeing Kingfisher, Grey Wagtail, even Dippers or Water Voles. Otter traces have been spotted. Turn immediately right over another style, leading into a large rough meadow, with Ox-Eye daisies, and many butterflies including Meadow Brown, Common Blue, Marbled White and Skippers. Garden Warblers sing in the scrub, and there is a chance of Nightingale and Grass Snakes.

Follow the well-worn path with the stream on your right. The Alders have Redpoll and Siskin in the winter. Cross the waymarked gates and continue straight, uphill. Blackcaps nest, there are a variety of ferns, and many spring flowers on the damp verge. Slant right at the track, with Thrushes, Wild Privet and more Traveller's Joy, then left at the main road, following it back round to Yetminster station.

REFRESHMENT
The Railway Inn at Yetminster, by the station. The Chetnole Inn.

$$\boxed{3}$$

SHERBORNE

HOW TO GET THERE
Sherborne railway station is on the south side of the town, just off Gas House Hill. There are often spaces to park in the streets by it, or there is a Pay and Display car park signposted close by.
OS Explorer Map 129. Grid reference: ST641162.

LENGTH
5 miles.

THE WALK
From the station turn right over the level crossing, then immediately left along the marked footpath beside the river Yeo. There is a chance

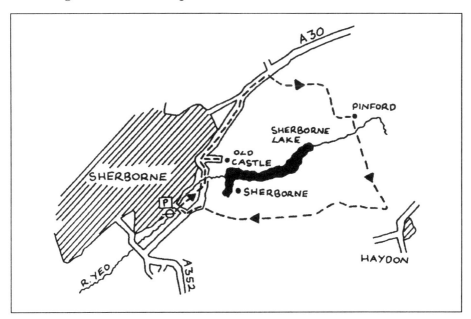

of Kingfisher, Grey Wagtail and even, rarely in winter, Dipper. The river is lined with thick clumps of Comfrey, Iris, Water Forget-Me-Not, and there are many Yellow Water Lilies. The Alders have Siskins and Redpolls in winter, Chiffchaffs and nesting Spotted Flycatchers in summer. Where the path rejoins the road, turn left over the railway.

On the second right is the road to the Old Castle, which is worth a visit, and offers the chance of scanning Sherborne Lake with binoculars for interesting waterfowl. In winter there are sometimes Goosander, and other unusual Duck, as well as Cormorants. Return the way you came and turn right up Oborne Road. There is Ivy-Leaved Toadflax in the old walls, together with Red Valerian, which attracts Peacock, Tortoiseshell and Red Admiral butterflies. On the right some barns have the openings that mark ancient pigeon lofts. Where the country opens out, there are Buzzards – and occasionally Hobbies – overhead. The hedge has Wild Privet, clouds of Hedge Bedstraw, Mallow, Woodruff, Wild Rose.

Turn right on to the A30, walking along the pavement. At Old St Cuthbert's Chancel, on the right, cross the road and follow the footpath sign. Go under the railway bridge, and over the waymarked gate straight in front. Cross the field diagonally to the left (east), cross the waymarked stile, then head straight through the next field. There are Skylarks in the grass, Yellowhammers and Whitethroats in the hedge, and large flocks of Fieldfare and Redwing in winter. Pass through the gate and up to the stile into the wood. Behind are views over both castles.

Follow the path veering right through the wood. There are Speckled Woods and possibly other woodland butterflies, Tawny Owls, Woodpeckers, Tits, Blackcap and Garden Warbler. In places the smell of Fox is very plain. The woodland floor is thick with Dog's Mercury, Redcurrants grow, as does Traveller's Joy in the clearings. Where the path crosses the track, continue straight over, watching for Pyramidal Orchids, Scabious, Lady's Bedstraw, and Greater Knapweed. Turn left to Pinford then turn right down the marked footpath just past the cottages. The bridge over the stream gives fine views of Teasel, Willow-Herb, and the chance of Kingfisher, several species of damselfly, including Azure, and Hawker and Emperor dragonflies.

Continue straight up to the tall gate into the deer park. There are herds of Fallow Deer, including white ones, Horse Mushrooms in the grass, and the possibility of Little Owls and Purple Hairstreaks in the Oak trees. Cinquefoil and Self-Heal are common, and the long grass encourages many butterflies, including Ringlet, Common Blue, Marbled White, Large Skipper, and huge numbers of Meadow Brown. Continue straight up the hill, watching out for free-range Guinea Fowl round the house. Pass through the tall gate and continue straight through the woods, with many Pheasants, including a few dark Japanese ones.

At the track turn right, then left, then right again, following the way-marks through mixed woodland called The Camp, with numerous Coal Tits, Goldcrests, and Sparrowhawk. Skirt a large barn to the left, following the signs, then swing right back through a gate into the deer park. There are more Fallow Deer, and Common Valerian grows in the Bracken. Pass through another gate, by the thatched gatehouse, and continue straight along a well-marked track. There are fine views over the new castle, and the lake. The open fields are sometimes edged with a mass of Field Forget-Me-Nots. Stock Doves and Thrushes are frequent in the isolated trees.

Where the track divides, take the marked footpath on the left, through the kissing gate. There are closer views over the lake, and with binoculars several waterbird species can be easily identified – Grey Heron, Mute Swan, Great Crested Grebe, Canada Geese, and the chance of more unusual visitors like Barnacle Goose and Ruddy Duck. Pass through another gate at the top of the hill, then follow the path swinging left along the side of the hill. At the end of the field, cross the road to the right, and go down Gas House Hill to return to the station.

REFRESHMENT
The Pageant Inn is close beside the railway station.

4

LYDLINCH

HOW TO GET THERE

From the A357 west of Sturminster Newton, take the turning off in Lydlinch signposted to Lydlinch church. There is a parking area a little way down on the right.

OS Explorer Map 129. Grid reference: ST743135.

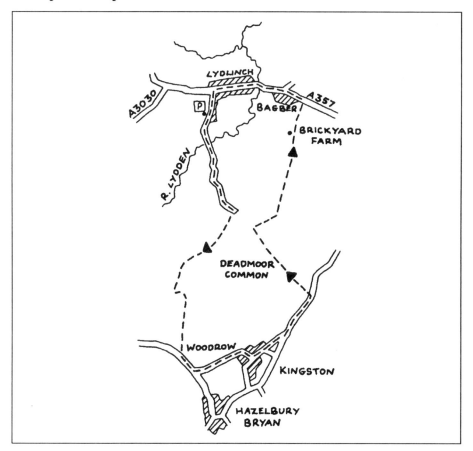

LENGTH

About 9 miles. Best in spring and summer.

THE WALK

Walk on down the lane past the church. There are old oaks, which are worth checking for Purple Hairstreaks, and the verges are thick with Teasels, Thistles, Fleabane, and other plants that attract butterflies. The bridge over the River Lydden gives views of many common waterside plants, including masses of Marsh Marigold. Dragonflies include the Brown and Southern Hawkers, and the fairly unusual Migrant Hawker. Grey and Pied Wagtails are frequent, and Green Sandpipers have been seen in winter. Watch for large flocks of Redwing and Fieldfare in the open fields between October and April. The broad verges have a variety of plant species, and attract several sorts of Grasshoppers. Wheatears pass through in spring and autumn.

At the turning to Holebrook Farm fork left, then at Holebrook Green Farm, where the road ends, take the gate on the right, opposite the farm entrance. Walk straight, with the hedge on your right. There is a pond on the left with Moorhen and visiting Herons. Warblers are frequent in the scrub. Go through the gate at the end and continue straight, with the hedge on your left now. Holly Blue butterflies haunt the Ivy. Gradually swing diagonally to the right (south-west), to the far corner of the field, go through and into Rooksmoor Copse, a typical wet woodland of the area, dominated by Oak and Ash, with occasional large Field Maples. Roe Deer are common, with their tracks everywhere.

The path leads straight along the edge of the wood. There are Long Tailed Tits, Woodpeckers, and huge stalks of Honeysuckle and Ivy climbing up the trees. Continue straight up the ride, with the possibility of Silver-Washed, Marsh and Small Pearl Bordered Fritillaries and White Admirals. Speckled Wood butterflies are everywhere, plants include Scabious, Tormentil, Self-Heal, and occasional Orchids. Where the ride meets Ridge Drove track at right angles, turn left. There are swathes of Water Mint and Gipsywort in the damp soil. Swing right through a gap between high hedges, then continue straight (south), past the waymark post. There are Cuckoos and Warblers in spring and Emperor dragonflies hunting in August. Keep straight on to the lane, then continue to the road at Woodrow.

Turn left at the road, then left again at the next junction. The road passes over a small stream with a thick cover of old Hazel coppice. The hedges have Bryony. Continue through Kingston Cross, swinging left again, then continuing left on the main road. Village gardens often attract Comma, Peacock and Red Admiral butterflies. The hedge is spotted with plants of fragrant Box. There is also Holly, Hazel, Traveller's Joy, and Honeysuckle.

Just past the right turn to Fifehead Neville, turn left up the lane by Elm Tree Cottage. At the end of the lane, turn right along the footpath, through more Hazel coppices, with the banks lined with Ferns and Dog's Mercury. There is an active Badger sett on the right. Deadmoor Common is a rich environment, providing a mixture of wet broadleaf woodland, dominated by Sallow and Blackthorn, and open clearings, which attract many butterflies, including Gatekeeper, Small Copper, Skippers, as well as other insects, notably Hornets (which despite their fearsome appearance are not at all aggressive). This is one of the best places in Dorset to hear a Nightingale singing in May. Garden Warblers and Lesser Whitethroats also nest. It is also the only place in the county to see Brown Hairstreak butterflies – look for the elusive golden-coloured females in autumn on Blackthorn.

Continue straight along the path, forking right. Watch for several species of Orchid. Foxes are common. Turn right along the track (Haydon Lane) through the reeds (if you reach the bridge over a stream, you have gone on a little way too far). Continue straight along the track, watching for grassland butterflies such as Ringlet, Wall, and Common Blue. At the junction turn left up another track. The verges have Grasshoppers and Crickets, including the Brown Bush Cricket. Hoverflies are attracted by flowers. There are Water Striders on the puddles. Turn left at the signpost to Brickyard Farm and continue on up the lane. Goldfinches and Swallows are common round the farm, and there is a pond on the left. Turn left at the main road, and follow it through Bagber back to Lydlinch. The double bridge gives more good views over the River Lydden, with Waterlilies, Demoiselle damselflies, and waterside birds. In Lydlinch pass the Deer Park pub, turn left at the sign to Lydlinch church, and return to the car park.

NOTE

The footpaths around Lydlinch are not particularly well signposted, and it is advisable to have an Explorer series 1:25,000 map. Waterproof footwear is essential.

REFRESHMENT

The Deer Park inn at Lydlinch.

5

FIDDLEFORD

HOW TO GET THERE

From the A357 east of Sturminster Newton, turn off by the sign to Fiddleford Manor. There is a free car park down the road on the left. OS Explorer Map 129. Grid reference: ST802136.

LENGTH

About 6 miles.

THE WALK

Come out of the car park and turn left up the road, then left again by the signpost to Sturminster Newton. Pass through picturesque Fiddleford Mill, and over the lock and the weir on the River Stour. There are Yellow Waterlilies, Bogbean, many fish, and waterside birds including Heron, Moorhen, Pied and Grey Wagtails. Watch for the pale White-legged damselfly, only found in Dorset in the upper Stour Valley. Turn

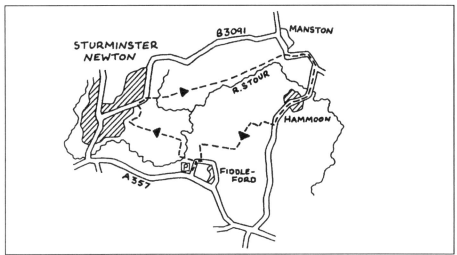

right, following the signpost to Sturminster Newton via Railway Path. Walk up the path with the river on your right, over a waymarked little bridge and stile. Tansy grows thickly. This stretch of river often has the earliest Swallows and Martins in north Dorset. Watch for the fast declining Water Vole.

Turn left along the railway line. Alder Buckthorn attracts butterflies. The old railway is marked by a fine line of Poplars which attract Poplar Hawk moths in late spring. There are many Rabbits in the surrounding fields. Warblers call from the scrub, and the Oak saplings have Oak Apples on them. Swifts fly overhead. Plants include thick Elder bushes, St John's Wort, and Tormentil. After the line crosses a bridge, turn right down some steps, then branch right to a gate into a new housing estate, where Lavender and Buddleia attracts autumn butterflies including Comma.

Continue straight, and at the end of the road turn right along the Manston Road. Where the road swings left, take the footpath on the right, signposted to Manston. Cross well waymarked stiles and a bridge, where the ditch is thick in Hemp Agrimony and Watercress. On the right are fine views of Hambledon Hill, where Oliver Cromwell defeated a Dorset uprising in 1645. The hedge is full of Rabbit holes, and their remarkably unwary inhabitants.

Follow the signpost to Manston Church, straight over the large hilltop field – not diagonally left towards Manston Copse, where Buzzards nest. Clouded Yellow butterflies and migrating Wheatears pass through in autumn. Green Woodpeckers hunt for ants' nests. There are sometimes Stonechat in winter. Cross over a small brick raised way, then a 3-bar gate and waymarked stile, continuing straight with a broken old hedgerow on your right. There are excellent views in all directions, and the River Stour is visible in front. The large field has Mushrooms, Common Spotted Orchids, and Water Dropwort. Halfway along the fence at the end, cross a waymarked stile, then continue straight over the next field, past a waymark post, reaching the edge of the river, lined with Iris, Purple Loosestrife, Marsh Marigold, and old Willows. Herons and Cormorants search out fish. There are Yellow Waterlilies everywhere. Kingfishers pass by, winter can bring a variety of Duck, in spring and autumn occasional Yellow Wagtails and Common Sandpipers pass by, and there is even a small chance of seeing one of Dorset's slowly increasing population of Otters. Dragonflies and damselflies can be very good, including Emperor, Brown and Southern Hawkers, the unusual Ruddy Darter, and Demoiselle damselfly. There are Frogs in spring, and the chance of a Grass Snake.

Turn out of the field to the right, by an old barn, continue up the lane, then turn right along the road over Manston Brook. Bats of several species often hunt this area. Kestrels cruise over the fields, and Goldfinches are common on Thistles. Follow the road, then turn right, signposted to Hammoon. The bridge over the Stour gives good chances of watching Trout and other fish. The road here sometimes floods in late winter, and there can be rarities, such as Goosander, in hard winters. Wild Geese and Bewick's Swans have been seen overhead. Continue straight through Hammoon, following the signpost to Okeford Fitzpaine.

A little way beyond the village turn right by the signpost of a bridle-way to Fiddleford. The fields often have Snipe and Lapwing in winter. Turn left by the waymarked signpost, and follow the path with the hedge on your left, keeping an eye open for Spotted Flycatchers. Go through the waymarked gate at the end, and watch for Grasshoppers and Crickets in the rough grass. There are usually Whitethroats and Yellowhammers in the scrub. Turn right along the disused railway line, by the signpost. There are massive displays of Thistles and Teasels in autumn. Toadflax grows in clumps. Turn left at the next signpost, and go down the lane. At the road turn right, then left by Fiddleford Mill, then right again to return to the car park.

REFRESHMENT
The Fiddleford Inn.

6

BULBARROW

HOW TO GET THERE

There is a large parking area just by Bulbarrow, on the Okeford Fitzpaine-Melcombe Bingham road. Views are superb.
OS Explorer Map 117. Grid reference: ST783059.

LENGTH

About 7 miles. Best in summer.

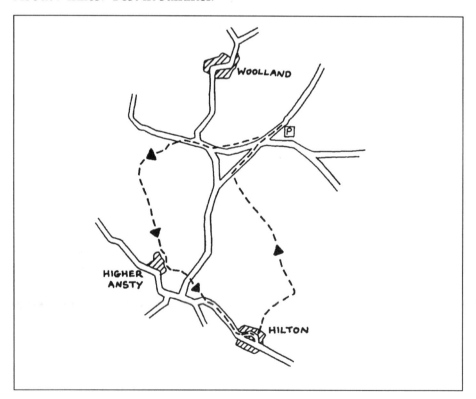

THE WALK

The Blackthorn scrub around the parking area attracts Warblers in spring, including the Garden Warbler, and sometimes migrant butterflies, including Painted Lady, in late summer. From the parking area turn left, then right and right again following the signpost to Mappowder. On the right is Woolland Hill picnic area, with scrub that can also be good for Warblers in May, and patches of Ling Heather that flower in August. Grasshoppers are numerous, and flowers include Harebell, Lady's Bedstraw, Wild Basil and Lesser Calamint. Continue past the area of forestry, following the sign to Stoke Wake. Kestrels hover on the hillsides. Butterflies include the Chalkhill Blue.

Turn left by the Bridle Path sign. Flowers include classic chalk grassland-loving plants such as Stemless and Musk Thistles, Rock Rose, Pyramidal Orchid, Eyebright. Swing left under the top of Rawlsbury Camp, and through the waymarked gate. Willow Warblers are numerous in the bushes, Green Woodpeckers hunt for ants. The Gorse has Green Hairstreaks, and there are Small, Grizzled, Dingy and Large Skippers, as well as Wall butterflies on the barer areas. Follow the path round the shoulder of the hill, then through the waymarked gate, and swing left downhill.

The woods have nesting Buzzards, Nuthatch and Treecreeper, and there is a good chance of watching Roe Deer from above. Continue straight down through two waymarked gates (these are not marked Wessex Ridgeway), and follow the track. There is a pond with Frogs, Newts, Common Blue and Blue Tailed damselflies, and Pond Skaters. Continue along the lane, beside an ancient hedge, with Hazel, Holly and Dogwood, through the farmyard, and on into Ansty.

In the village fork left, then turn left at the T-junction and continue through a waymarked gate, and along a woodland path among Ferns, and old coppiced Hazels – worth checking for signs of Dormice, and for the parasitic Toothwort. Jays are frequent, and Holly Blues haunt the Ivy. Fork right and emerge into an open field. Head diagonally left (south-east) to where the old broken hedgerow meets the main hedge, where there is a small waymarked gate. Go through and cross straight over the road over a waymarked stile. Cross over the field diagonally to the left, cross another waymarked stile, and then continue diagonally right to the gate on to the road.

Turn left and continue along the by-road into Hilton. The hedge is rich in Bittersweet and Traveller's Joy, while Squirrels hunt for Hazelnuts in the autumn. The wood on your right has Dog's Mercury, Bluebell, Violet, Wayfaring Tree, and Tawny Owls. Continue into Hilton, following the main road round to the left (the church on the right is usually locked, but has an interesting 1690 sundial outside). Turn left by Hambledon Cottage, signposted Bulbarrow, and continue straight up the track where the road swings left. There are an interesting variety of Ferns in the shade, Wild Privet in the hedge, and the open areas are rich with flowers in summer, including Knapweed, St John's Wort, Ox-eye Daisy, Scabious, Harebell. Butterflies include Common and Holly Blue, Brown Argus, Marbled White, and Brimstone.

Near the hill top, where the main track swings right, turn left by the waymark, and then go through on to the open hillside, with the hedge immediately on your right. This is the old Drove Road. On the edge of the field are a rich assortment of cornfield weeds, including Scarlet Pimpernel, Field Pansy, Poppy, Corn Chamomile, Field Forget-Me-Not, Mayweed. There are masses of Foxgloves in the hedge, butter-flies including Small Heath, Meadow Brown, Gatekeeper, and superb views to the left. Finch and Bunting flocks are numerous out of the breeding season. Buzzards hunt over the rough grassland, and some-times it is possible to see five or six in the air at the same time. The rare Red Kite has been seen in winter. Foxes and Rabbits are often easy to see. The thick areas of Gorse are worth checking for Green Hairstreaks, and look for Nettle-Leaved Bellflower. Giant Puffballs grow in early autumn. Spotted Flycatchers nest in the trees, and Whitethroats in the Blackthorn scrub.

Continue straight along the drove track until you reach the road. Turn right here along the edge of Delcombe Wood, with a fine display of mature Beech trees. In winter Bramblings have been seen in mixed Finch flocks feeding on the Beech mast. Where the roads meet, the car park is straight ahead.

REFRESHMENT
The Fox at Ansty.

7

PLUSH

HOW TO GET THERE
Park on the broad verge by Folly Farmhouse, halfway between Piddletrenthide and Mappowder.
OS Explorer Map 117. Grid reference: ST728033.

LENGTH
About 6 miles. Best in summer.

THE WALK
Take the eastern bridleway signposted to Dorset Gap, on the far side of the road from the farmhouse. The high hedges have Willow Warblers, Tits, Speckled Wood butterflies, and Ferns. There are Dark Bush Crickets in the grass verges. Just before the waymark post, fork right. Southern Hawker dragonflies sometimes patrol the area. Go through the gate and follow the old track as it veers up to the right. You are on an area of chalk grassland and scrub, with Field and Devil's Bit Scabious, Carline Thistle, Eyebright, Harebell. Butterflies include

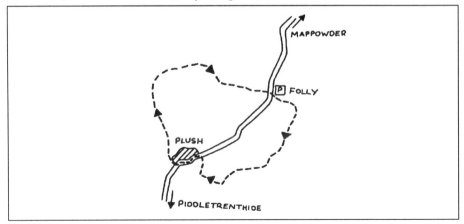

Skippers, Small Copper, Brown Argus, Small Heath, and the chance of a Dark Green Fritillary. Goldfinches are common on the varied species of thistle, and Linnets and Yellowhammers nest.

Continue straight along the track. At the waymarked gate, do not go through, but turn right, with the hedge immediately on your left. There are excellent views over the surrounding countryside. The wood on the left was once coppiced, and has a variety of common woodland birds, including Woodpeckers and Tawny Owl. Continue, with the triangulation point on your left. Skylarks are frequent above. The massive stands of Ragwort are sometimes stripped by huge numbers of black and gold Cinnabar moth caterpillars. In winter the fields sometimes have Lapwing, and occasionally Golden Plover, flocks.

Go through the waymarked gate at the end of the field, then head diagonally right across the field, to the edge of the copse, then swing sharp right to the waymarked gate. Quail have been heard calling in these fields. Go through the gate, and continue straight. Plush is visible at the bottom of the hill, almost straight ahead.

Cross the waymarked stile, then head diagonally right, down a faint track, to the bottom of the hill. Go through the gate, then turn left on the road into the pretty and well-kept village of Plush. The bird tables of the village attract a variety of visitors, including Tits, Finches, and once I saw a bold Brown Rat feeding there. Turn left at the Brace of Pheasants inn, then right at the gate, marked with a waymark to Alton Pancras.

Continue up the fairly steep shadowed track, with Dunnock, Dog Rose, Robin's Pincushions, Holly trees and Violets. Emerge on to Watcombe Plain conservation area by a gate with two waymarks on it. Follow the one that points straight, not to the left. The ancient strip lynchets are plain to see. Migrant birds can be seen here in spring and autumn, including Wheatear and Whinchat.

This is another stretch of chalk grassland, and as it has free access, it is worth taking time to explore. There are Marbled White, Blue and Skipper butterflies, and plants such as Self-Heal, Devil's Bit Scabious, Tormentil, and Eyebright. It is worth looking on the edge of the steeper slopes for Wild Thyme, Milkwort, Rock Rose, and there is a chance of Bee Orchid or Autumn Gentian. Meadow Pipits are frequent, there are several species of moth, and Clouded Yellow butterflies visit. Flocks of Redwing and Fieldfare visit in winter.

At the waymark post at the end of the field, slant right until reaching the hedge, then continue with the hedge on your left. The hedge has a rich display of Blackberries and Foxgloves, and Primroses in spring. At the ancient, grass-walled enclosure, follow the path forking right. There is a chance of hunting Hobbies overhead between May and August, and Little Owls have been seen near the woodland edge. Passing the Wessex Ridgeway waymark, enter a ride with woodland on either side. There are good chances of seeing a Silver Washed Fritillary, Painted Lady, or Comma on Brambles, Purple Hairstreaks can sometimes be seen high around the branches of Oak trees. Buzzards nest in the wood, and often hover over the hillsides. This is a good area to watch for hunting Stoats and Weasels.

The woodland is old Hazel Coppice. There are many signs of Badger activity, it is worth checking for evidence of Dormice, and Jays are frequent. In autumn there is a rich variety of Fungi, including a few Boletes, and Toothwort sometimes grows around the old Hazel stools. Flocks of Tits with Nuthatches and Treecreepers are frequent in winter. Cross the waymarked stile on the left and then continue straight with the hedge on your left. The grass is often beaten down by the Roe Deer, coming out of the woods.

Continue downhill through the rough scrub. The Gorse bushes are worth checking for the elusive Green Hairstreak. There is a variety of Grasshoppers and Crickets in the long grass, and Stonechats can be seen outside the breeding season. Holly Blues flutter round Holly and Ivy.

The path goes back into woodland, with more Hazel, Ferns, Dog's Mercury and Bluebells. In spring Blackcaps sing. Traveller's Joy grows thickly where the path emerges. Follow the narrow lane back to Folly, watching out for black Peacock caterpillars on the Stinging Nettles.

REFRESHMENT
The Brace of Pheasants at Plush.

8

BROWNSEA ISLAND

HOW TO GET THERE

Boats visit Brownsea Island from Poole Quay regularly from April to September. There are also occasional boats from Sandbanks, Swanage and Bournemouth. There is a landing fee for non-National Trust members.

OS Outdoor Leisure Map 15. Grid reference: SZ032877.

LENGTH

About 3 miles. Good all year, but between October and March the only visits are generally by recognised organisations such as the Dorset Wildlife Trust.

THE WALK

From the jetty, follow the sign to the church, with the castle on your left. On the right is a hide looking out over the lagoon, and the neighbouring marsh. This is one of the prime places for bird-watching in Dorset, and almost anything can turn up at the right time of year. There is a heronry, which famously now includes breeding Little Egrets - the first place they have ever bred in Great Britain. The Egret nests are not visible from the public hide, but the birds themselves are nearly always present and hard to miss. There are also nesting Gulls and a Sandwich

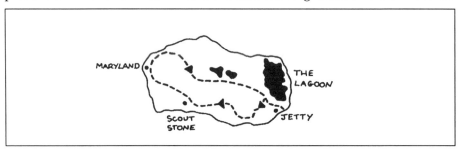

and Common Tern colony. The flock of several hundred wintering Avocets begins to arrive in early autumn and rapidly builds up, while large numbers of Cormorants and Oystercatchers also gather. Spoonbills visit regularly, and sometimes Ospreys will stay for a few days in the autumn. Likely waders include both Godwits, Redshank, Greenshank, Dunlin, and usually others. Shelduck are always present, and in spring and autumn there are Teal, Wigeon, and other species. The marsh shelters Reed Warblers, Water Rail, and a few Water Voles. There are sometimes Oyster Mushrooms on the trees close by.

Continue on, through a mixture of trees including Laurel, Yew and Spanish Chestnuts (which are numerous on the island), then take a left turn, signposted to the South Shore. The open grass has Peacocks, Pheasants, Rabbits, and Puffballs. Continue on, then swing left following another signpost to the South Shore. Do not go down the steep steps to the beach, but swing right, signposted Cliff Walk and Viewpoint. At the next junction turn left for a fine view over the southern half of Poole Harbour, then bear right back inland past a huge old Monterey Pine. Turn left and continue on to return to the main path. There are large Holly bushes worth investigating for Holly Blue butterflies.

Turn left and follow the signpost to the Scout Stone. Opposite the Visitor Information house, the heath begins on your left. Nightjars do nest on the woodland edge, but day visitors are highly unlikely to see or hear them. Woodcocks too tend to be elusive, but at the right time of year there is a better chance of seeing Grayling, Green Hairstreak and Fritillary butterflies. Just past the Scout Stone, fork right along the southern edge of the heath. In autumn there is a varied collection of fungi, including some dramatic Russulas. The pine trees have bat boxes on them.

Continue straight, then swing right by the open grass with pine trees and fungi underneath them. At the signpost, continue on to Maryland, then swing round to the right. There are fine views west, towards

Wareham. Spotted Flycatchers often visit these trees. Continue round to the right, through a mixture of pines, rhododendron, and birch. The pines have numerous Coal Tits and Goldcrests, and several species of fungi, including Inocybes, underneath. Near a large Virginia Creeper plant is a turning left on to a stony beach, with more views over the harbour. In spring and autumn there is a good chance of Mergansers, Eider Duck, and Grebes, including the Slavonian and Black Necked.

Return to the path, which swings round to the right, and through a deer fence. Notice how the area inside the fence is regenerating much faster and more thoroughly than that outside it, with many saplings. There are some fine stands of Scots Pine, and in the autumn there is a good chance of seeing Red Squirrels, Brownsea's most celebrated inhabitants anywhere between here and the Nature Reserve entrance.

Take the left turn, signposted to the Quay, and continue straight. There are some old Beech trees on the right, which sometimes attract autumn finches, and yellow puffballs grow beneath them. The invasive Rhododendrons, attractive in May, provide concealment for a few of Britain's most exotic birds, the Golden Pheasant, which despite the male's astonishingly brilliant colours, is shy and hard to see. Continue straight until you reach the old vinery wall, then turn right and go down to look at the pond, which has waterlilies, ducks, and dragonflies. This is also one of the best places to see both Red Squirrels, and the island's Sika Deer. Return back up to the main path, and follow the signs back to the Quay. On the left is a water-logged wood, with Sallow and Alder and nesting Ducks and Moorhen. On the right are more Beech trees. Watch for unusual fungi in autumn. Birch trees sometimes have the rare dark orange Cortinarius purpureobadius underneath them.

On the left is the entry to the Dorset Wildlife Trust reserve, with a nature trail that non-members can follow for an additional charge. It includes a visit to several splendidly situated hides in the very heart of the lagoon. Continue on straight, back to the landing place. A check on the surrounding water may well reveal Sea Duck, Guillemots, or Grebes. The boat trip back usually includes a cruise round some of the other islands.

REFRESHMENT
There is a National Trust tea shop close by the quay.

9

CRANBORNE COMMON

HOW TO GET THERE
Alderholt is between Fordingbridge and Cranborne. On the west side of the village, near the Churchill Arms pub Ringwood Road leads south off Station Road, the main through road. Turn up Ringwood Road and park behind the Post Office.
OS Outdoor Leisure Map 22. Grid reference: SU115124.

LENGTH
7 miles. Best in summer and early autumn.Waterproof footwear advisable.

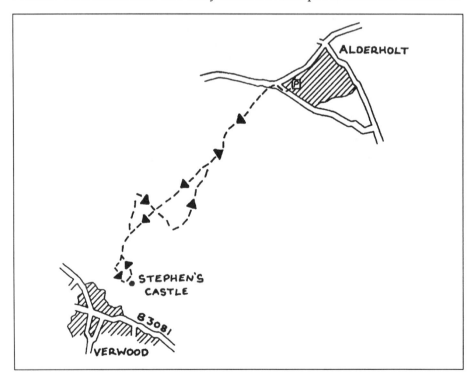

THE WALK

Return up Ringwood Road, turn left into Station Road, then almost immediately left again into Blackwater Grove. Go straight down the road, then continue along the waymarked Bridleway at the bottom of the road. The track is surrounded by a mixture of trees, including Oak, Pine, Holly and Birch, and is a good spot for Tit flocks, and sometimes more unusual birds. In autumn there is a variety of fungi, including Honey Fungus and Sulphur Tuft on tree stumps. The rough grazing on the left is popular with Rabbits, and occasional hunting Foxes. Continue straight as far as the gate marked Private, then swing left along the main track. Jays are frequent in autumn, and there are often Pipits.

Turn left by the waymark and the sign for Cranborne Common Nature Reserve, then almost immediately right by another waymark. The path is fairly boggy. Abruptly the scene opens out into a wide stretch of open wet heathland, dominated by Cross-leaved Heather, and grasses and sedges. Look for the attractive Bog Asphodel, and dragonflies. Curlews have been known to nest. Follow the blue-painted posts across the Heath, which grows higher and drier, with sand underfoot, small Pine saplings, and more Ling Heather and Gorse. Stonechats are always present, and butterflies are good, with all the browns, including Grayling, as well as Silver-Studded Blue, and Large and Small Skipper.

Continue straight, following the blue posts. On the edge of the heath, and in the nearby woods there are fungi, including several species of Bolete. Continue straight into the plantation ahead (with the firebreak a few yards away on the right) looking out for Coal Tits, Goldcrests. Crossbills have been seen here, and in winter there is a chance of Siskin and Redpoll flocks. The path swings left, then crosses another Bridleway. Continue straight over the ride, with the transmitter on your left. The path then swings right to join an unsurfaced road.

At the next bridleway junction, turn left and continue straight, following the waymarks. The Bracken-cloaked slopes on the edges of the rides attract Tree Pipits in summer, while Woodcock can be seen at dusk, especially in the winter. There is also a chance of Nightjars on the woodland edge. Continue straight past the barrier, and the signpost to Verwood.

A little way further on, turn left by the sign marked Footpath Only, and climb straight up on to Stephen's Castle, with Ling and Gorse, and fresh opportunities to see the dry Heathland species of bird, butterfly and especially reptile. Snakes are often seen in March or early April, warming up in sunny hollows. Follow the small path, and turn right at the T-junction with another path, then left and follow the line of the fence, with excellent views south.

Descend the steep steps that lead off Stephen's Castle, and turn right along the sandy track downhill. In autumn magnificent Fly Agarics are frequent by the path, and there are patches of Sphagnum Moss dotted with Sundews. On the right is a wide area of wet moorland, with Cotton Grass, and a rich variety of dragonflies, including Black and Common Darters, Hawkers, Hairy dragonfly, and the dramatic Emperor and Golden-Ringed.

Turn left along the large unsurfaced road, and continue straight into the wood, going uphill, with Tormentil and other acid-loving plants on the edge of the road, and a fine variety of pink and purple Russula fungi in the autumn. Turn right along the waymarked bridle path, watching out for Woodpeckers, and the dramatic orange, but deadly poisonous Cortinarius speciosissimus mushroom. Hornets have been seen here, and it is worth keeping an eye open for White Admirals in July, around Honeysuckle plants. You are retracing part of the path you took before.

At the next Bridleway junction, turn left and follow the blue arrow posts. There are Crickets in the pathside grass, Squirrels and Deer. Turn right at the next junction, past a barrier, and continue straight, with the transmitter on your right, passing immediately under the telegraph wires, not swinging right with the larger track.

Roughly 100 yards further on, by a cluster of Holly trees, turn left down a small path. After perhaps 20 yards the path seems to be blocked by barbed wire, but on the left is a yellow-painted stile. Cross it and follow a small, twisty path, marked by occasional trees with yellow painted rings on them, that runs along the edge of some open wet heath, with the main wood immediately on the left. This stretch is popular with Green Woodpeckers hunting for ants. Pass between two yellow-ringed trees back into the wood, and continue straight, over the forest track. Ahead is another stile, a Nature Reserve sign, and a view over Cranborne Common. In winter there is a chance of a wandering Hen Harrier, and a Great Grey Shrike has visited. In summer Hobbies hunt for dragonflies.

Turn right, then immediately left, and strike across the heath by the yellow post. The Gorse bushes on the right are often a good spot for Stonechats and Dartford Warblers. Reed Buntings are frequent in the boggier areas. Continue along the small path, which is marked by occasional yellow posts. Where the yellow posts meet the blue ones, turn right and follow the blue ones. From here on you are retracing your steps back to Alderholt by the way you first reached Cranborne Common.

REFRESHMENT
The Churchill Arms pub is on the edge of Alderholt.

10

WAREHAM FOREST

HOW TO GET THERE

On the north side of the Wareham – Bere Regis road, about one mile out of Wareham, are signs to the Sika Trail. Turn off and park in the sign-posted Parking.

OS Outdoor Leisure Map 15. Grid reference: SY906895.

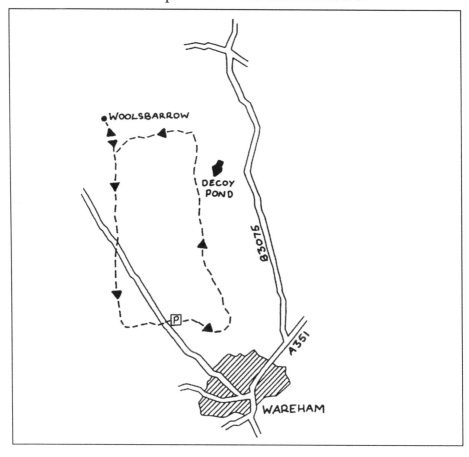

LENGTH
About 8 miles.

THE WALK
Take the main Sika Trail, marked with red-circled posts, to the right from the car park. The forest here is a mixture of Heather and Scots Pine. Foxgloves are numerous, and autumn fungi include the Blusher, and the large, handsome Boletus pinophilus. Look in the trees for Crossbills, Redpolls and Siskins. Continue following the red-ringed posts, swinging left at the end of the wood. Black Darter dragonflies are numerous in autumn. The Heather is a mixture of Ling, Bell, the paler Cross-leaved in wetter areas, and rare Dorset Heath.

Continue following the red-ringed posts first right, then swinging left round the edge of the wood. Spiky Lycoperdon puffballs are fairly common. On the right is an area of boggy Bramble brakes and Sallow and Alder carr, which attracts Warblers. Firecrests have been known to nest. Roving flocks of Tits, sometimes accompanied by Nuthatches or Treecreepers, hurry through the trees. The golf course to the right is often visited by Rabbits, and flocks of migrating Wagtails and Pipits.

Beyond the golf course, the area on the right opens out into a large area of wet heath, one of the largest such regions in England, with Heather, Bilberry, Cotton Grass, Bog Asphodel, and the stunning Marsh Gentian. Reed Buntings nest. The ponds have a huge variety of dragonflies, including the heath-loving Small Red damselfly, Four-spotted Chaser, and the unusual Hairy dragonfly. It is also worth looking for Marsh Grasshoppers and Bog Bush Crickets. Under the pines are large yellow Suillus Variegatus fungi. There is also a chance of the weird-looking Fir Sponge, a bit like a cauliflower, that grows around pine trees, and many other autumn fungi. A few stands of Hemp Agrimony attract butterflies.

By Parson's Pleasure, where the Sika Trail and the red posts go off to the left, continue straight, noticing the interesting variety of conifers on

45

the left. Continue straight north through the gate, with open heath on both sides. The drier areas have Stonechat, Dartford Warbler, and in spring there is a chance of seeing reptiles sunning themselves, including the rare Smooth snake. Look for Silver Studded Blue and Grayling butterflies, and the handsome Emperor moth. Nightjars are perhaps the best attraction, and a visit to the forest edges of heathland clearings in late June, perhaps an hour after sunset gives a good chance of hearing them churring, or their sharp cries as they swoop around like huge bats in pursuit of moths. Woodcock and Little Owls can also be seen at dusk. During the day, especially in spring, it is worth keeping an eye and ear open for the rare and declining Woodlark.

Continue on through another gate, back into woodland. The Decoy pond is away to the right, and sometimes attracts birds such as the Little Grebe, and even (rarely) Osprey. The whole area of the heath offers the chance of hunting Hobbies in summer. In winter it is bleak, but there are sometimes Hen Harriers and Peregrines, and Great Grey Shrikes have been seen a few times.

Pass under the electricity pylons, then at the next gate turn left and follow the track. There are more unusual mushrooms under the trees. Escaped Cotoneaster plants have established themselves. Grey Squirrels and Roe and Sika Deer are present, but sometimes shy. Keep following the main track, until it swings left (south). The hill fort at Woolsbarrow is up on the right, and worth a detour for its excellent views over the surrounding area. Return along the path from Woolsbarrow and follow the path with the Wareham Forest Way waymark. The Downy Emerald dragonfly can be found around here. The path crosses a patch of sphagnum moss with sundews. Sandier stretches offer the chance of reptiles, and Tiger beetles.

Continue straight, following the waymarks, and crossing a marked bridge. The ground has a rich variety of fungi, including several sorts of Russula, and Bolete. Sparrowhawks hunt the clearings. The path emerges by a caravan site, follow the right-hand edge of the site, then turn right by the waymark on to the road. Cross the road, turn left, then immediately right along the waymarked path, which emerges on to a stretch of heath where ponies are often grazed.

Turn left by a waymark, then swing back round to the right by another waymark, following the path beside a fence on your left. The wood, with Oak, Sallow, Birch, Honeysuckle and Bryony, has a good variety of spring flowers. Flocks of Tits and Thrushes are frequent. Turtle Doves have been seen. Butterflies may include the White Admiral. Continue along the path, which becomes hemmed in by high Gorse hedges – many of its branches have the bright orange Tremella mesenterica fungus growing on them. Turn left by the yellow waymark (before reaching the electricity pylons), following the line of a large old hedgerow. Continue straight across on re-entering the forestry area, then swing left towards the road and the entrance to the Sika Trail on the far side of the road.

Cross the road and walk back to the car park. On the way watch out for the solitary Eucalyptus tree on the right, and some magnificent Fly Agaric fungi on the left by the road.

REFRESHMENT
The Silent Woman pub at Coldharbour, just up the road from the Sika Trail parking.

11

CHRISTCHURCH HARBOUR

HOW TO GET THERE

From the A35, close by the station, follow the signs to Southbourne and the Southbourne Beaches. From Belle Vue Road, turn left along Broadway, following the sign to Hengistbury Head. There is a long stay car park at the end of the road.
OS Outdoor Leisure Map 22. Grid reference: SZ163912.

LENGTH

About 4^1/$_2$ miles round Hengistbury Head. A further 1^1/$_2$ miles around Stanpit Marsh. All year (but can be crowded in summer).

THE WALK

At the Head Ranger's Office by the car park leaflets on the area are available. Follow the path straight, then turn right, following the sign-

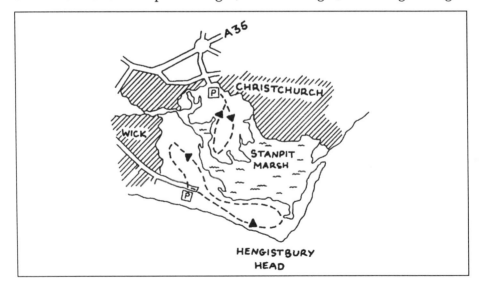

post 'via Cliff top'. The rough grassland has Rabbits, Skylarks, Meadow Pipits and Linnets constantly present. Watch on the Gorse for Stonechats and the chance of a Dartford Warbler. Follow the metalled by-road up to the Iron Age fort at the top of the head, with magnificent views over Christchurch Harbour, and the sea. Sea watching on the head can yield a rich variety of seabirds in spring and autumn, including Gannets and Skuas, Seaduck, Auks and Grebes in winter, and occasional sightings of Bottle-Nosed dolphins. The groynes on the beach sometimes shelter wintering Purple Sandpipers, and usually have Cormorants perched on them.

The wildlife ponds are there to encourage dragonflies and amphibians. The heath beyond is a mixture of Marram Grass, Heather, and different varieties of Gorse, as well as small Holly bushes. Butterflies include the Dark Green Fritillary, Green Hairstreak, and Grayling. Rare birds, such as Hoopoe and Wryneck, turn up every year during migration.

Take the steps down, with a mixed woodland dominated by Rhododendron and Scots Pine on your left. Swing left round the back of the beach huts then continue straight along the south shore of the harbour. On your left are ponds with Alder, Birch and Sallow, on your right saltmarsh with Teal, Wigeon, Redshank, Curlew, Oystercatcher, Godwits, Shelduck, Heron, occasional Little Egrets, and Kingfisher, Brent Goose and Goldeneye in winter.

The wood you enter is dominated by scrub Oak, with occasional Yew and Holly. Bluebells in spring. There are several species of Tits, and Great Spotted Woodpeckers raid the nest boxes. Watch for Fritillaries, Purple Hairstreaks are worth searching for in the upper branches of Oak trees, there are plenty of Oak Apples to be found, and a rich variety of moths are present, including most interestingly the Broad Bordered Bee Hawk moth. Further on the woodland has a variety of exotic escapes in it, including Bamboo, Cherry Plum (flowering as early as February), Jasmine Box, and Cherry Laurel.

You now emerge by a stretch of reedbeds, which offers the chance of Bearded Reedlings in winter, and Sedge and Reed Warblers in summer. Sparrowhawks hunt over the area. Just before the Golf Course, fork right on to a path and follow the signpost 'Wick via Fields' through a gate. On the right is a patch of Wild Lupins, on the left clumps of Teasel. New ponds are being dug, and Willows planted. Fork right, heading for the church, over the meadows, which are rich in flowers in spring and summer, including Marsh Marigold and Ragged Robin. Green Woodpeckers search out ants' nests.

By the signpost marked 'Holdenhurst 4', turn sharp left, then fork left again so you are heading back towards the Head again, with a fence on each side of you. Foxes are common round here and can often be smelt! Turn right by two huge logs, watching out for some unusual Thistles. Go through the gate, then left along a metalled track, before turning right again by a chicken wire fence. Go straight over the Golf Course, (a good place for seeing Wagtails) and find yourself back at the car park.

Drive back to the A35, then follow signs to the Leisure Centre. Park at the Pay and Display by the Centre, Grid ref SZ167927 and take the path out on the left (the opposite side to the Centre). Follow it through marshy woodland, with Woodpeckers, and a fine display of Yellow Iris in May. Having crossed the stream, turn right and follow the line of the hedge straight down to the edge of the nature reserve, with a caravan that sells leaflets and has a board telling you what can be seen that day.

Having turned right, past the caravan, continue straight on to Stanpit Marsh. The freshwater sections have many plants, including Water Crowfoot, Water Mint, the handsome Flowering Rush, and Marsh Marigold. Cetti's Warbler is often present. Further out, you get views over the harbour, with Grebes, Coot, and many species of Duck in winter, as well as Heron, Little Egret, and summering Terns. Dartford Warblers visit, and unusual migrants such as Grey Phalarope (especially after autumn storms) and Kentish Plover (usually in spring) are almost commonplace. Almost every year the area picks up at least one species of American Wader, and this is one of the best places in Dorset to find Jack Snipe.

Follow the track round to the right. The saltmarsh has Thrift, Eelgrass and Glasswort (often called Samphire, and very pleasant to eat raw). In winter it is possible to get within a few yards of the large flock of wintering Brent Geese, and Teal, Wigeon, Curlew and other winter visitors are often unusually confiding. Look out for Godwits, Grey Plover, There is a large Gull and Wader roost that is always worth checking for surprises. At the gate, fork left, follow back to the bridge, turn left and make your way back to the car park.

REFRESHMENT
Christchurch is a charming town, with a rich variety of pubs, restaurants and cafes, as well as the impressive Christchurch Priory, which is well worth a visit. The fish on the church weather vane is a reminder that Christchurch used to be an important Salmon run.

12

GARSTON WOOD/ PENTRIDGE

HOW TO GET THERE

From the A354 take the B3081 to Sixpenny Handley. Turn right then right again, following the signs to Bowerchalke. Drive up the road about 1¹/₂ miles, and turn in by the RSPB Garston Wood sign, and park there.

OS Explorer Map 118. Grid reference: SU 004195.

LENGTH

About 8¹/₂ miles. Best April to September.

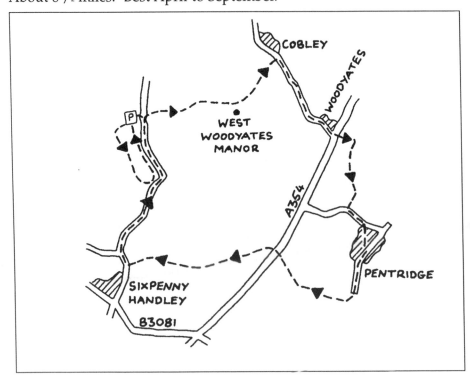

THE WALK

Walk into the RSPB reserve and take the path to the right of the reserve sign. Garston Wood is a mixture of Hazel coppices, Oak and Ash, with some large old Whitebeams and Field Maples. The woodland floor in spring is a mass of flowers, including Ramsons, Primrose, Violets. In summer it is possible to find Valerian, Columbine, and orchids, including the Greater Butterfly. Two parasitic plants, the Bird's Nest Orchid and Toothwort, both occur. Woodcock visit in winter. Continue straight, then about 100 yards before the gate turn left.

Walk straight through the wood. In spring and summer listen for the soft call of the Turtle Dove. There are Nightingales, Lesser Whitethroats and Garden Warblers in the coppices, and Dormice too, though you are very unlikely to see any. In winter and early spring the Hazel debris has fine examples of the declining, bright orange cup fungus, Sarcoscypha coccinea. Oak trees may have Purple Hairstreak butterflies in their upper branches. Follow the path as it swings left round the edge of the wood, through a sea of Bluebells. In summer keep an eye open for White Admiral and Silver-Washed Fritillary butterflies. The Pearl-Bordered Fritillary is possible. Nuthatches, Treecreepers and Great Spotted Woodpeckers are often seen, as are Squirrels. By the gate turn left again and continue straight northwards. There is Woodruff and Wood Spurge on the woodland floor. By the wooden bench, turn right, and continue straight, with the hurdles on your right. Finally turn right back to the car park.

Go on the road, turn left, then right by the footpath waymark. Continue straight, with the fence on your left. These fields are often used by Roe Deer, Foxes and Partridges. The strip of woodland on the left has Bluebells, and a variety of shrubs including the spiny-leaved evergreen, Butcher's Broom. Where the path is crossed by another track, turn left – the path swings right again. Yellowhammer and Linnets are frequent. Continue straight along the path to the north side of West Woodyates Manor, but do not go into the farm, instead turn left with a hedge on your right. The crop fields are popular with Crows,

Woodpigeons and Stock Doves. Follow the path past the signpost to Cobley with the woodland edge on your right, then across the field to the gate.

Turn right down the by-road, noting marks where Badgers dig for worms. There are several species of shrub in the hedge, including Holly and Wayfaring Tree. Continue down into Woodyates. The village gardens attract butterflies such as Peacock, Small Tortoiseshell, Red Admiral. Cross the main A354 and follow the waymark to Bokerley Farm opposite. (Continuing straight here will lead you to the Martin Down nature reserve, with its open grassland, rich variety of butterflies, and the chance of unusual birds such as Stone Curlew – which nested a few years ago – and Hobby.) A hundred yards further on, turn right by the gate, along a marked bridle path. There are Skylarks and Red Legged Partridges in the fields. Brown butterflies in summer, including Small Heath. Follow the track, which turns into a twisting path with trees and bushes on either side, including Dogwood. Sparrowhawks hunt the area, and Hobbies are occasional. Where it meets another path, turn right.

At the road, turn left, then just before the sign of Pentridge, go through a waymarked gate on the right. Outside the breeding season watch for flocks of Finches and Buntings. Go round the right hand side of the field, and go through the first gate on the right, by Pentridge church and its award-winning wildlife churchyard. Continue to the road, then turn right by a clump of Teasels. Follow the road through Manor Farm yard. There is a small stream on the right that has attracted Yellow Wagtails in passage time. Turn right by the waymark, then right again, so that the hedge is on your right, and continue straight up the hill. There is a variety of cornfield weeds on the field edge, Quail have been seen or (more likely) heard. Barn and Little Owls hunt at dawn and dusk, and winter Thrush flocks can be large. Watch for Marbled White, Common Blue and perhaps Grayling butterflies. Continue by the side of the field, down the hill and across the old Roman Road, and then by the garage over the A354. Pass through the gate marked The

Hardy Way, and with the fence on your right, swing round to the left. There are Snowdrops and Hedge Garlic in the hedge. Wheatears pass by in spring and autumn, and the fields have abundant Skylarks and Pipits, and sometimes Lapwing and Golden Plover in winter. Watch out for Hares. Continue straight, past some bee-hives, crossing a by-road, and continuing straight on through a waymarked gate.

Swing right (north-west) towards the buildings, continue straight past the water trough, and go through the gate at the end and take the track. Turn right on to the road, then right again, following the signpost to Bowerchalke. The road is lined with scattered Beech and Oak. There are Deer tracks everywhere. Pheasants include the dark Japanese Pheasant. Walk up the side of Garston Wood, watching out for Woodpeckers, Goldcrests and flocks of Tits. The bank on the right has Wood Anemones and other spring flowers. Finally turn left back to the car park.

REFRESHMENT
Pubs in Sixpenny Handley.

13

COMPTON DOWN/ASHMORE

HOW TO GET THERE
From Shaftesbury take the B3081 signposted Tollard Royal, then after a mile and a half turn right, then right again, to Melbury Abbas. Drive through the village and on south towards Fontmell. Stop at the Parking on the right with fine views to the west.
OS Explorer Map 118. Grid reference: ST886187.

LENGTH
About 9 miles. Best April to September.

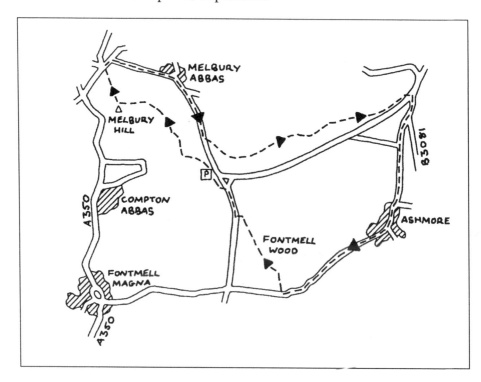

THE WALK

Take the lane on the right of the parking, with rough grassland falling away on the left and hedges cloaked in Traveller's Joy on the right. Foxes hunt here for numerous Rabbits, and Sparrowhawks for small birds. There are Violets on the ground, and a quarry on the left with some interesting chalkland plants. Turn right by the waymark up to Compton Down and follow the path as it swings round to the left. There are fine views, and plants include many Carline Thistles, as well as Lady's Bedstraw, Bird's Foot Trefoil, Salad Burnet, Thyme, Rock Rose. Continue along the path as it swings right round the shoulder of the hill. Butterflies are excellent, among the best in Dorset, and include Marbled White, Skippers (especially the rare Silver-Spotted), Small, Common, Chalkhill and (the fast-declining) Adonis Blues, Brown Argus, Grayling, and Dark Green Fritillary. Clouded Yellows and Painted Ladies are often present in autumn.

Cross another track, and then head straight up towards the top of the hill. Meadow Pipits and Skylarks are everywhere. Keep an eye open for several species of Orchid, including Bee Orchid, as well as the rare Clustered Bellflower and Early Gentian. Slant left by the fence, amongst Gorse and Blackthorn to the triangulation point at the top of Melbury Hill. There are fantastic views in all directions. Migrating birds, especially Swallows, Martins and Wheatears, can be seen on some spring and autumn days. Raptors include Kestrel, Hobby in summer, while one or two Hen Harriers have been seen in winter.

Cross over the waymarked stile behind the hill top and continue straight down, with some Bracken scrub away to your left. Cross another stile and continue down over some managed grassland, via two gates, to reach the road by a telephone box. Turn right along the road, then 200 yards on right again down Quarry Lane. The hedges here, honeycombed by Rabbit holes, have a good variety of the commoner wayside flowers, such as Campion, Celandine, Cuckoo Pint, various umbellifers, and Orange Tip butterflies. Finches and Tits feed. Holly and Ivy plants attract Holly Blue butterflies. Come into Melbury Abbas with the church on your left, and turn right on to the larger road, through the village. At the end of the village is a small woodland area with Snowdrops, Ferns, and a variety of fungi. Walk up the hill, past a variety of shrubs including Honeysuckle, Wayfaring Tree, Guelder Rose.

Beyond the top of the hill, take the left hand stile marked National Trust Path. Follow the line of the hedge (on your right) with fine views over Melbury Down below you, and Melbury Wood on the far side of the valley. Mushrooms are common in the grass, while Fieldfare and Redwing feed on the Hawthorn in winter, and Stonechats nest in the Gorse, where Green Hairstreak butterflies can be found. Pass over several stiles, keeping the fence on your right, and pass a spinney of Scots Pines with Pheasants, then continue over more stiles. Buzzards soar overhead, Hare, Fox, Fallow and Roe Deer are frequently seen on the woodland edge. The scrub sometimes has Nightingale, Garden Warbler, and even Grasshopper Warbler.

Finally reaching the road, turn left, then right by the signpost to Tollard Royal, then right signposted to Ashmore. The line of Beeches has clumps of Snowdrops underneath in early spring. Partridges (mostly Red-Legged) and Pheasants are frequent in the fields, as are huge flocks of Crows outside the breeding season. Continue straight through Ashmore, turning right by the village duckpond (with Geese and Mallards), and walking between the Wesleyan chapel and the church. Continue out of the village and downhill. Winter thrushes are numerous on the fields, Goldfinches feed on Thistles, while winter Finch flocks sometimes include Redpoll. The Conifer plantation on the right has Tits, Goldcrests.

At the bottom of the hill, turn right by the signpost to Blandford-Shaftesbury road into Fontmell Wood. Broad-Bodied Chaser dragonflies are occasional. There is Wood Anemone, Hazel coppices, Wood Spurge, Mullein. Roe Deer are numerous. Great Spotted Woodpeckers, Goldcrests, Treecreepers and Nuthatches are often visible. Blackcaps and Turtle Doves can be heard in summer. Further into the wood, where there are more Beech trees, spring sees great swathes of Ramsons and Bluebells, as well as clumps of Primroses and Ferns. Sparrowhawks hunt. Watch for Duke of Burgundy, Silver Washed Fritillary and White Admiral butterflies. White Hygrophorus fungi can be seen in autumn.

On seeing a gate in front of you, go through it on to the main road and turn right. Walk up the road (or possibly just inside the edge of the wood). After the second turning right to Ashmore and Compton Abbas airfield, cross the road and walk along the path on the left hand side of the road, with views over Fontmell Down, back to the car park.

REFRESHMENT
Pubs at Fontmell and Tollard Royal.

14

UPTON HEATH

HOW TO GET THERE

From the main A35 dual carriageway, follow the signs to Upton Country Park. There is ample parking at the Park.
OS Outdoor Leisure Map 15. Grid reference: SY992930.

LENGTH

About 6 miles. Good all year.

THE WALK

From the car park go back to the entrance to the park, then turn right by the entrance, parallel to the road, with Upton House on your right. There are a good variety of shrubs and trees along the track, including

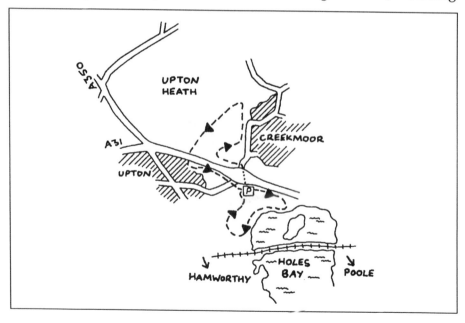

some rare examples of full-grown Elms. Watch for Small and Large Skippers and Wall butterflies. Turn right by the cycle path to Poole signpost, and continue through Silver Birch and Holm Oak, with drifts of Campion in early summer. Larger Oaks attract Purple Hairstreaks. Holes Bay is directly in front.

Holes Bay has a rich variety of bird life, especially at migration times, and in winter. Teal, Wigeon, Shelduck, Curlew, Black-tailed Godwit, Oystercatcher, and Redshank are all numerous, and rarer species, such as Ospreys, sometimes turn up. Turn right through the gate in a high fence into Upton Country Park (open 9 to dusk), and walk parallel to the shore. Buzzards can be seen overhead, there are Teasels, and the pond on the right has Iris; dragonflies such as the Emperor, Four Spotted Chaser, and Southern Hawker, and Duck, often including Teal. Green Woodpeckers hunt for ants in the grass.

Continue along the path. There is a hide on the left, with more views over the salt marsh. Ruff and Kingfisher visit in winter. Tits are fre-quent in the Blackthorn. Follow the sign marked Shoreline Trail, through some Alders, which attract Siskins. Go through the gate, past some Scots Pines. The fields have wintering Thrushes, and Stock Dove. Bluebells grow among the Elder, Beech and Holly. Further on is a line of Willows, and some reedbeds. Brown Argus butterflies have been seen.

Turn right at the stream, through another gate, and on straight. The wood is dominated by Rhododendrons, which look dramatic in May, but also has many Foxgloves. Go through the gate, then turn right, signposted Broadstone. There are some fine Cedars, and a small lake with Coot, Moorhen, Amphibious Bistort, dragonflies. Squirrels raid pine cones.

Turn left by the pond, then right (not left along the broadwalk), then left by the gate marked No Cycling. The path twists through Holly, Laurels, Beech and Rhododendrons, keeping the fence on your left.

Garden Warbler and Lesser Whitethroat are possible. Great Spotted Woodpeckers are frequent, Lesser Spotted Woodpeckers have been seen, and Starling and Redwing flock in winter. Go through the gate, and turn left to return to the car park (on the right is a rebuilt Romano-British farm).

Continue up the road, out of the country park, and cross the road straight in front. Follow the sign to the left, marked Castleman Cycle Path. Go round to the right, and go under the A35, then follow the cycle path over two roads, and under a footbridge. Here, go straight ahead into the wood, mainly Scots Pine, which has attracted Crossbill. Follow the track over a small stream as it bears slightly right, then turn left by the Permissive Path waymark. Swing right by the next waymark, among younger conifers on the heath edge, then right by another waymark, swinging round between the woodland edge on the right and the heath. Common and Silver-Studded Blue butterflies are possible. Adders bask in sunny spots in spring. Firecrests have been seen. Go through the old fence, then turn left through wet woodland dominated by Sweet Chestnut and Beech. Follow the signpost Roman Road. Gorse attracts Green Hairstreaks.

Just past the first electricity pylons, turn left along a well-worn path. Roe Deer are frequent here. The path swings right, with an extensive area of wet heath on the left. Among the birds that can be seen are Curlew, Nightjar, Sand Martin, Tree Pipit, Dartford Warbler, Redpoll, Reed Bunting, Snipe and wintering Jack Snipe. The nationally rare Scarce Blue-Tailed and Small Red damselflies are present, as are dragonflies including the Ruddy and Black Darters. Keep on the left-hand path and go up a steep slope on to a track. Turn left along the well-marked track on the top of the ridge, following the dismantled railway. There are many ponds down on the right. Watch for the Emerald damselfly. As the track approaches the A35, it swings right up on to a footbridge on the left. Use this to cross the road.

Go down off the bridge and along the path with the dual carriageway immediately on your left. Keep taking the left hand path, until it curves round on to a road in a housing estate. Follow the road, then take the first left and continue straight on as it swings round to the right. At the end, turn left, under an arch by number 107, and cross the stile in the corner into Upton Wood.

Follow the path to the left, keeping an eye open for Blackcap in the trees. After the small plank bridge, take the central path straight ahead. There is Water Starwort in the water, Marsh Thistle and Gladdon close by. Silver-Washed Fritillaries visit the wood in late summer. Swing left, through the Rhododendrons, and then follow the path to the corner of the wood, with a roundabout in front of you. Cross over the stream on the left, then take the path on the right on to the road. Cross the road and follow the Upton Country Park signs back to the car park.

REFRESHMENT
The Upton Country Park Heritage Centre, with displays about the area, also includes a café.

15

HOLT HEATH

HOW TO GET THERE

From the A31 east of Wimborne, take the turning to the north sign-posted Holt, Broomhill. At Broomhill turn right, signposted Whitemoor, Mannington. Turn right by the sign to the National Nature Reserve and park there.

OS Explorer Map 118, & Outdoor Leisure Map 22. Grid reference: SU048036.

LENGTH

5 miles. Best in summer and autumn. Waterproof footwear strongly recommended.

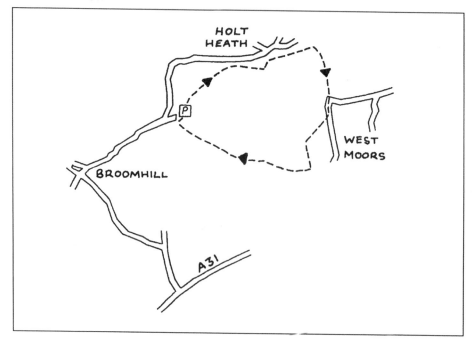

THE WALK

From the car parking area, walk back towards the entrance, then right by the blue waymark. Walk through the Birch wood. On the left the heath opens out with scattered Scots Pines and Gorse. Buzzards hunt overhead. Continue straight at the next waymark. On the right the heath is being gradually restored. There is a rich mixture of Heather, which cloaks the area purple in late summer, including Cross-leaved Heath, which prefers wetter situations. Look for the thin red stems and pink flowers of the parasitic Dodder. The Scrub Oaks have Oak Apples, each of which may contain up to 30 larvae of a Gall Wasp. Wrens are frequent in the Gorse, and are sometimes mistaken for Dartford Warblers. Skylarks sing overhead. Silver-studded Blue and Grayling butterflies can be seen.

Continue straight along the main bridle path, with boggy areas. There are fine views over the heath, with the chance of unusual raptors such as Merlin or Hen Harrier in winter. The Gorse may hide Dartford Warblers, and will certainly have Stonechats and Green Hairstreak butterflies. Holt Heath is one of the best heaths in Dorset, and flowers include Bedstraw, Tormentil, Heath Spotted Orchid, and Bog Asphodel in wetter areas. The sandier areas show interesting beetles, and there is a chance of any of Britain's six reptiles, most probably the Adder basking in sunny hollows in March or April.

Go right along the Permissive Path through Birch and Silver Birch. Pipits are present. There are ponds on the left which give the chance of several dragonflies, including the Broad-Bodied Chaser, Black Darter, Keeled Skimmer, and Emperor. Turn left at the T-junction, then almost immediately right by the Public Bridleway signpost, along a small track. This opens out into a grassy ride by the back of some gardens, with a rich display of spring flowers, including Bluebell, Primrose, Celandine, and many true Wild Daffodils, far smaller and more delicate than garden escapes. Brimstones appear in early spring. Finches are frequent in the trees, and there may be Warblers in summer.

Turn left at the by-road, then right opposite the thatched cottage, by the Holt Heath NNR sign. Then turn left by the next track, back on to the open heath. Continue straight, with more chances of Dartford Warblers. This is the only place in Dorset where Curlew nest regularly. Kestrels hunt, Hobbies pass over in summer, the rare Great Grey Shrike has been seen in winter. Continue straight up hill, then swing right on the ridge, with Scots Pines on your right, on the top of the hill. Turn right on to a bigger track, then continue as far as the low electricity pylons. Sundews grow in patches of Sphagnum Moss, and Snipe can be seen drumming in spring. Have a look at the pond on the right, then return to the main track.

By the gate turn right, and follow the twisting track through a wet strip of woodland, with Holly, Oak, Silver Birch, Ferns, and many ponds. Damselflies include the rare Small Red. Redwing and Fieldfare visit in winter, as do Redpoll. There is an interesting variety of fungi, including the Razor-strop fungus. Where the Birch-dominated woodland becomes Pine-dominated, there is a chance of Crossbills in autumn and winter. Banks of moss are brilliant green even in high winter. Continue down the path, with fields on the left, lined by willows where Little Owl has been seen.

Where the track meets the by-road (Newman's Lane), continue straight ahead, then turn right by the blue waymark, and immediately left through a very wet area. Grasshopper Warbler and Reed Bunting nest. Slant left by the waymark back on to the heath, then follow the permissive path that runs under the pylons. Stonechat is frequent in the Gorse. There is a burnt area on the right, which is beginning to regenerate. Just past the burnt area, turn sharp right by the waymark along the edge of the wood, with the burnt area on your right again. Continue along the path through a rich mixed woodland. Some of the fire-scorched Pines are recovering. Tit flocks often visit the area. Cross the stream and follow the blue arrow though a mixture of Silver Birch and Oak. Watch for White Admiral butterflies in July, and there is a chance of both Small Pearl-Bordered and Pearl-Bordered Fritillaries.

Where the waymark points left, continue straight then slant left along the open ride. The conifer plantation is lined with Red Oaks, which provide a mass of colour in autumn. Foxes often hunt round here, and I once saw one carrying a dead Turkey. Cross the stile and continue straight. This area is being gradually reclaimed for heathland, and ponies now graze it. As the view opens out, there is another chance of heathland specialities. Green Woodpeckers hunt out ants' nests, Tree Pipits visit in summer, Woodcock are occasional. The Woodlark has been seen. Continue along the track, with good stretches of Heather on the left, and a conifer plantation on the right, where it is sometimes possible to hear, or more rarely see, Nightjars on summer evenings in June and early July. The plantation is thick with fungi in autumn, including several species of brightly-coloured Russula. Go through the gate at the end, and then continue straight uphill, noting invading Rhododendron on your right. The Pines have large numbers of Goldcrests and Coal Tits, and a chance of Siskins and Crossbills. The car park is on the right.

REFRESHMENT
The Barley Mow pub is on the Colehill Road between Broomhill and Wimborne.

16

HURN

HOW TO GET THERE

Take the B3073 to Hurn. At the roundabout, take the turning to Sopley, then turn immediately left, signposted Matchams. Drive up the road for about 2 miles, and park on the left, by the Forestry Commission, Matcham's Lane.

OS Outdoor Leisure Map 22. Grid reference: SZ128989.

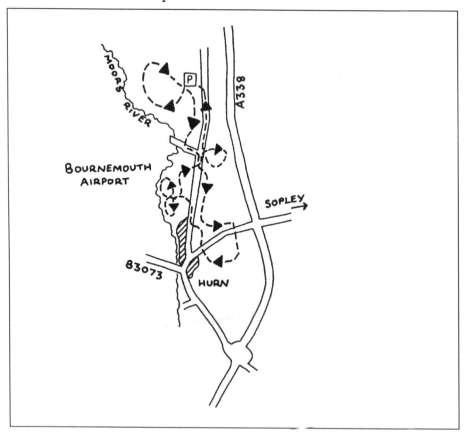

LENGTH
About 6¹/₂ miles. Best April-October.

THE WALK
Go through the main gate along the track at right angles to the road, among Pines. The inconspicuous Spring Beauty flowers on the ground. In the autumn there are a variety of fungi. Continue straight for a short distance, then turn left along a track that leads out on to open heathland. Turn right and continue up the open area, going straight past the CAC Parking sign, then turn right again at the next place where tracks cross. This is a good place to see Dartford Warblers. Adders often doze in early spring sunshine. Follow the track back into the forest, then turn right again along the main track, and follow it back to the car park.

Just before the car park, turn right and walk along the trail parallel to the road. Pheasants are frequent. Tits (including Marsh Tit), Treecreepers and Goldcrests hunt in the trees. Opposite Portview Caravan Park, the path swings right, then follow the Permissive Path waymark to the left. Follow the blue-painted posts, among numerous Foxgloves, into an area that has been felled, with a view over Bournemouth Airport. On the road, turn right and walk down for a look over the reed beds around the Moors River, where there are Sedge and sometimes Reed Warblers in summer, then return up the road, with open heath on your right, overrun by Rabbits.

At the main road, turn right, and walk along the verge, which has Bluebells, Daffodils, and Bryony in the hedge. Cross the road and go through the gate on the left that leads into the wood, and turn immediately sharp right, parallel to the road. Long Tailed Tits are frequent in the Birches. There is an interesting variety of conifers, including Cedars and one or two Redwoods. Stonecrop grows on open ground. Turn left on to the Dorset Wildlife Trust nature reserve of Sopley Common.

Follow the path straight through a mixture of Heather, Birch, Gorse, and Pine, with sand underfoot. Green Woodpeckers are common,

Lesser Spotted Woodpeckers less so. Gradually the path swings left then right, with the heath growing wetter, and more dominated by Cross-leaved Heath. There are areas of Sphagnum Moss, with Sundew, Cotton Grass, dragonflies, and the large, yellow-striped Raft Spider. Follow the path up on to the partially bare sandy ridge, with extensive views eastwards. Turn right and follow the ridge. Like other areas of dry heath, this provides the possibility of Sand Lizard and Smooth Snake. Insects include the rare Heath Grasshopper, Green Tiger Beetle, Grayling, Silver-studded Blue, and Sand Wasp. Descend diagonally to the left by a steep and narrow, but well-marked path, coming down to the road. The woodland edges have Nightingale, Nightjar, Woodcock, while fungi include Fly Agaric, Ink Cap, and Boletes. Go left along the road a short distance, then right (south) by the DWT sign along a by-road. Follow the by-road, then turn right uphill through the wood, turn right again along a sandy track with a picnic area on the left, and return to the road.

Cross the road and re-enter Sopley Common by the reserve sign, with Bluebells. Listen for Lesser Whitethroat in scrub, and Bullfinch. Turn left, then right at Matcham's Lane. Walk up the road (north). Finch flocks sometimes include Redpoll. By number 122, turn left and follow the by-road as it swings left, then continue straight ahead, with a house (and small swimming pool) on the left. At the end of the track, by the barn, turn right through rhododendron bushes to the DWT Troublefield reserve sign.

Take the left hand path, through the gate by the WWF sign and out into a wet meadow. Plants here include Purple and Yellow Loosestrife, Iris, Water Mint and Hemlock Water Dropwort. Turn left and go along the edge of the field, then cross the ditch by the remains of a bridge, go round the southern field, then return over the bridge, walking by the side of the Moors River, which has Yellow Waterlily, Starwort and Arrowhead. There are several species of Fern, including the Royal and Lady, and the Broad-leaved Helleborine can be seen in shady areas in July and August. Visiting birds include Heron, Water Rail and Snipe.

Return through the gate, then turn left by the reserve sign and follow the path through wet wood of Sallow and Alder. Roe Deer are frequent. Enter the open area called the Paddock, with Devil's Bit Scabious, Lesser Skullcap, Marsh Pennywort. The rare Large Alder Sawfly has been seen.

Turn right, and cross the stile on the right, and then proceed to the river, where there is a riverside path. Turn left and follow it through thickets of Comfrey as far as the backwater, where it fades away. The undergrowth includes Guelder Rose and Alder Buckthorn. Chiffchaffs often winter. This is the best area for insects, including the Scarce Chaser, White-legged damselfly, and Dark Bush Crickets. Sadly the Orange-spotted Emerald dragonfly is now extinct here and in the whole of Britain. Retrace your steps back along the river's edge, reaching a rather battered stile. Cross over it (or beside it) back into the boggy meadow, turn left and return through the gate and back up on to the by-road.

Just past the house on the right, turn left through Pines, and out into more open land, with a line of old Oaks and a scattering of Holly trees on the left, Bracken on the right. Turn right by the sewage treatment works, then continue to the main road. Turn left along the road and walk up it (north). Just past the signpost to the Eastern Business Park, cross the road and turn left into the DWT HRZ reserve, with open heathland, more Roe Deer, and frequent Mistle Thrushes. Turn left then left again, then left again, so that you circle round in a loop, and emerge on the road where you left it. Turn right back on to the road, walk up it a little, then take the roadside ride on the left (western) side of the road, and so back to the car park.

REFRESHMENT
Just beyond the A338 is the Avon Causeway Inn.

17

MOOR CRICHEL

HOW TO GET THERE

From the A354 take the road signposted Moor Crichel, Horton. Turn right at the Horton Inn on to the B3078. Turn right signposted Witchampton, Moor Crichel. Continue into Witchampton, signposted Crichel, and park in the lay-by just beside the church.
OS Explorer Map 118. Grid reference: ST989064.

LENGTH

About 7 miles. All year.

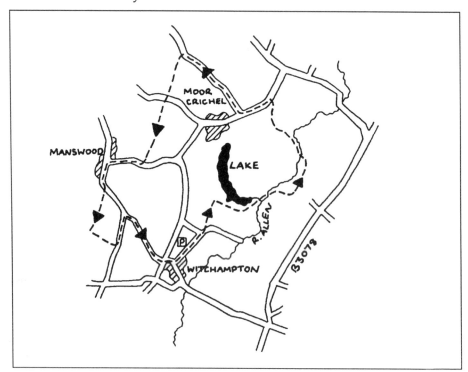

THE WALK

Walk on through the village, then turn right signposted Moor Crichel, the Gussages, with fine views over rolling countryside. The hedgerow has a variety of escapes, including Periwinkle and Oregon Grape. Follow the waymarked path through the fancy gate on the left into the parkland around Moor Crichel house, with a variety of trees including Smooth-leaved Elms, Cedars. Winter Thrushes frequent the area, and the parkland has Horse Mushrooms and Great and Lesser Spotted Woodpeckers. Follow the signposted footpath to the right. Crichel lake on the left is choked with weed in summer, but has a Gull roost, Tufted Duck, Cormorant, Canada Geese, sometimes feral Greylag and Barnacle, occasional Ruddy Duck, wintering Shoveler, and numerous Gadwall. A flock of Wigeon, uncommon in central Dorset, winters, and can be seen on the great lawns.

Continue along the path, with a backwater on the left sheltering Moorhen and Coot. The strip of woodland, with many Beech, has masses of Snowdrops, Primrose, Ground Ivy, Bluebells, Ferns. Go through the white gate, with the stream on the left and a ditch on the right thick with Watercress. The river edges have the poisonous Hemlock Water-Dropwort, and Water Mint. Herons are frequent, and Bitterns have been seen in winter. Watch out for Frogs, and Grass Snakes. The River Allen is now visible on the right. Bushes of Butcher's Broom and large numbers of Coltsfoot on the left. Demoiselles and dragonflies, including the Common Darter are good.

Cross the river, and follow the road round to the right, passing through the gate by Didlington Farm. Turn left after the barn, and continue straight (north) up the bridleway signposted Stanbridge. The attractive chalk stream is on the left, with Reed Buntings, Kingfishers, Grey Wagtail, Sedge and Reed Warblers, and in winter occasional Teal, Snipe and Green Sandpiper. Mandarin Duck have been seen. There are swathes of Butterbur. Go left over the bridge and along the track with the river now on the right. Turn left at the old mill and continue straight (west) up the hill. Kestrels hunt the fields, and there are Green

Woodpeckers. In winter there is a chance of Lapwing, Golden Plover, and Harriers and Peregrine occasionally hunt overhead.

The track swings right into a stretch of woodland, with Laurel, Ferns, Bluebells, Sweet Chestnut, varieties of fungi in autumn. At the road, turn left signposted Moor Crichel, Witchampton, with fresh views over rolling farmland and an avenue of Southern Beech trees down to the village.

Turn right along the by-road signposted Long Crichel. The verge has a good mixture of commoner wayside plants, including Celandine, Campion. Orange Soldier beetles are frequent on Cow Parsley, Orange Tip, Red Admiral and Small Tortoiseshell butterflies are often numerous. Watch for Partridges, Barn Owl. Fields of stubble attract finches and buntings. Turn left by the signpost Cock Road, crossing a small stream and following the route of an old Roman road up the hill along the woodland edge, with Ramsons and Bluebell. The conifer plantations attract Goldcrest, Coal Tit, Bullfinch.

Fork right then continue straight ahead (south), surrounded by Bluebells. At the road turn right, then perhaps 100 yards down the road, turn left by a wooden bridleway signpost, across an open field. Follow the path into an open woodland, which has many Roe Deer. There are Larches on the left, and some large Holly bushes which attract Holly Blue butterflies. Rough grass has Marbled White and Gatekeeper butterflies. Continue on to the small road, and keep straight (south). On the main road, opposite the old school, turn right, and follow the road. Goldfinches often visit the gardens. At the junction turn left, signposted Tarrant Rushton. Follow the road round. Yellowhammers are frequent. There are winter Thrushes, while Finch flocks occasionally include Tree Sparrow and Brambling.

Where the road continues swinging left, go straight on (south) by two waymarks. Oilseed Rape is much grown in this area, and this sometimes attracts Corn Buntings, and swarming Bees. Flocks of

Woodpigeon and Stock Dove can be very large. The stretch of wood on the right has many Bluebells. Mistle Thrushes nest. Turn left by the waymark, then continue straight (east). Wheatears are occasional visitors on passage.

At the road, turn left, then right, signposted Witchampton. Continue between hedgerows. The small stretch of woodland on the left, Downley Coppice, sometimes has nesting Buzzards. Dog's Mercury covers much of the wood floor. There is Wild Privet, Wild Rose, and more Bluebells. At the T-junction, turn left, then right down Pound Hill, then right by Ivy House towards Witchampton church. Go through the lych gate, looking at the attractive churchyard, with banks of Violet and Primrose. Go past the church (which has a fine Tudor brass), down the far side of the church, then turn right to the lay-by.

REFRESHMENT
The Drover's Inn at Gussage All Saints. The Horton Inn. Witchampton has a village store.

18

BADBURY RINGS/SHAPWICK

HOW TO GET THERE

From the A31, take the B3075 signposted Spetisbury, Blandford. At Spetisbury cross the main road and go straight over the bridge, signposted The Tarrants, Shapwick. Take the first right to Shapwick, and park in the centre of the village, near the Anchor pub.
OS Explorer Map 118. Grid reference: ST937018.

LENGTH

About 9 miles. All year.

THE WALK

Return along the road out of Shapwick (west), then continue straight along the waymarked track by Bishops Court Farm. Cross over the stile into the farmyard, then follow the path beside a small stream, with

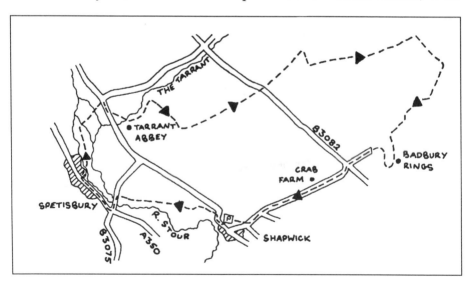

Moorhen, lined with Iris, and overhung by Alders. The path curves left over the stream, pass through a gate and cross the field to the right, following a waymark, to the stile on the far side. There are some fine old Oak trees, and Barn Owls have been seen in these fields. Cut across to the next stile, passing under the pylons, then go diagonally left to the next stile. The River Stour is on your left.

This broad stretch of the river attracts a variety of waterfowl, including, outstandingly for Dorset, small flocks of wintering Goosander. Canada Geese and Mute Swans are often present, as are Tufted Duck, with occasional Wigeon, Teal, Shoveler and Gadwall in winter. The bank is thick with Iris and Comfrey. Cross another stile and go straight through the middle of the next field to the next stile, emerging on the road. Turn left and cross the ancient Crawford Bridge, looking along the river. Wagtails are always present, Kingfishers sometimes. Cormorants fly over.

Go right along the pavement by the busy A350. There is a huge rookery on the left, high above Spetisbury, and views over the river on the right. Continue beside the road past the Baptist Chapel, then turn right down a small waymarked track, down to the river. Cross a footbridge, then swing left, following the river, which is lined with Willows and Alders. Kingfishers and Herons are possible throughout this area. Damselflies include the Banded Demoiselle, White-Legged, Blue-Tailed, and Common Blue. Follow the river as far as the telephone lines, then swing diagonally right (north), crossing a waymarked stile, and then a footbridge (with another footpath joining from the left). This area has begun to attract Little Egret, and Green Sandpiper sometimes winter. Continue straight (north), crossing a ditch, then another footbridge, and emerging along a by-road by the Keynston Mill Fruit Farm.

Turn right on the road, signposted Spetisbury, with an interesting verge, rich with wayside plants, including Violet, Bluebell, Honeysuckle, Primrose. Woodpeckers are frequent. Turn left by the footpath sign, and cross the field diagonally to the right (east), to the stile. On the by-road cross the River Tarrant, then swing left with Tarrant Abbey House on your right. The area is thick with Daffodils. The Tarrant Crawford church on your right has a churchyard with many Snowdrops, and fascinating medieval wall-paintings inside. Continue up the lane by the river, then turn right along a waymarked bridleway. Butterflies to watch out for include the Ringlet, Marbled White, Orange Tip, Brown Argus and Common Blue.

Walk uphill. The Cow Parsley attracts Orange Tip butterflies, and there is a Rabbit warren in the hedge, as well as clumps of Gladdon. Turn left at the next waymark along an old drove road. Foxes hunt here, and Badgers scratch up the earth. This area attracts Stonechats in winter, as well as Yellowhammer. Common Blue butterflies in summer. Continue straight (north-east), and cross the B3082, to the by-road opposite, signposted Witchampton. The path is just to the right of the by-road, and the fence is thick with Traveller's Joy. Turn right along another track, signposted Public Right of Way, then left, with Jubilee Wood on your right. The wood, a mixture of Hazel coppice, Ash and Elder, has Roe Deer, and a deserted Badger sett near the fence. Continue along the track (east). These high fields, with their wide views, attract Lapwing and occasional Golden Plover in winter. Skylarks sing constantly. The field verges have a variety of cornfield weeds. Stubble fields in autumn and winter attract large Thrush, Pigeon and Finch flocks. Tree Sparrows have been seen by the barns.

Where the road turns sharp left, go through a green gate and follow the footpath with the hedge on your left. Pass through the gate by the Kingston Lacy Estate sign, cross a waymarked stile by the Pater Noster Cross stone, then turn right down a by-road. By another Kingston Lacy Estate sign, at the edge of a wood, turn right and follow the track through the wood, which is carpeted with Dog's Mercury, has Tits, Great Spotted Woodpecker, Tawny Owl, Ferns, and some fine ancient Oaks. Follow the waymark straight over another track and continue south and downhill. Buzzards wheel overhead.

Pass through a gate and into Badbury Rings. Go left up a clear path on the edge of the Blackthorn-Hawthorn scrub, which is popular with Bullfinches. Swing right, then pass through a gate on to Badbury Rings proper, with more scrub and woodland. Watch for Brambling among the winter finch and bunting flocks. Butterflies include Brown Argus, Silver-washed Fritillary, Wall, Large, Small and Dingy Skippers, and perhaps the rare Silver-Spotted. Circle the area, then make your way down past the car park to the main road (B3082), which is lined with fine old Beech trees.

Cross over and go straight down the road opposite, signposted Shapwick. Fieldfare and Redwing winter in the fields. Kestrels hunt overhead. The Beech trees by Crab Farm often harbour Long-tailed Tits. Enter the village by the High Street, and by number 9 turn right by a Dorset County Council footpath sign. Cross a stile, then walk diagonally left (south-west) over two more waymarked stiles. Continue in the same direction to the next two stiles, by the farm buildings, and emerge on the road. Turn left and come back to your car.

REFRESHMENT
The Anchor Inn at Shapwick. The Drax Arms at Spetisbury.

NOTES